Introducing
of His Glory

Trevor Lloyd
Archdeacon of Barnstaple

Jane Sinclair
Lecturer in Christian Worship, St. John's College, Nottingham

Michael Vasey
Lecturer, in Christian Worship, Cranmer Hall, Durham

GROVE BOOKS LIMITED
Bramcote   Nottingham   NG9 3DS

CONTENTS

THE COVER PICTURE

is compiled from Christmas motifs

First Impression April 1991

ISSN 0305-3067
ISBN 1 85174 176 3

1. A WINTER DIRECTORY

by Michael Vasey

'The people who walked in darkness
have seen a great light;
those who dwelt in a land of deep darkness.
on them has light shined' (Is. 9.2)

For Christians in Northern Europe the celebration or commemoration of the incarnation has been bound up with people's experience of winter. The darkness of which Isaiah speaks is that of despair and estrangement. A rich interaction of popular and church culture have clothed and interpreted the images of light and darkness and used them to explore the scriptural themes of judgment and salvation, incarnation and revelation.

The Liturgical Commission's new book *The Promise of His Glory* provides a collection of material for use from autumn through to spring. Much, but not all, of it draws on the rich seasonal tradition that is influenced by the climatic mood of the period. *The Promise of His Glory,* commended by the House of Bishops on 16 October 1990 and published in July 1991, is an amended version of the Liturgical Commission Report GS907 published on 7 April 1990 under the same title.

History and authorization

Almost the only seasonal material in the Book of Common Prayer was the fine Collects and a few Proper Prefaces. Authorization for a more generous and creative approach to seasonal material had to wait for the Series 3 Holy Communion service (1973) with its much richer provision. A further step came in 1986 with the publication of *Lent, Holy Week, Easter.*

Some people may have been taken by surprise by the publication of *Promise.* There was no mention of a resource book for 'All Saints to Candlemas' in the Report *The Worship of the Church* (GS 698), a reworking by the Standing Committee of a draft report of the 1980-85 Liturgical Commission. This report, debated in General Synod in November 1985, recommended that the authorization for the ASB should be extended to 2000 and proposed a three-stage programme for the Liturgical Commission:

1. A programme of teaching and study backed by a 'directory' and other resource material

2. A thorough and sustained evaluation of the ASB 1980

3. The preparation, as circumstances require, either of additional material or of substantially new texts. (section 43)

(The term 'directory' points to a more flexible and pastoral approach to the ordering of worship; it had already been used in the Introduction to *Lent, Holy Week, Easter*). The two Reports *Patterns for Worship*[1] and *The Promise of His Glory* should be seen within this strategy. They are part of a process of exploration by which the Church of England discerns the way worship is to be ordered and resourced beyond 2000 AD.

[1] GS898 (CHP, Published 30 November 1989). See also Trevor Lloyd, Jane Sinclair, Michael Vasey, *Introducing Patterns for Worship* (Grove Worship Series no. 111, Grove Books, Bramcote 1990).

Full Synodical authorization is a lengthy affair governed by the strict rules of English Church law; it recognizes the doctrinal sensitivity and unifying power of liturgical texts. Careful following of these procedures for the ASB has established agreed patterns and prayers for central elements in worship and also ways of handling controversial doctrinal matters. There are considerable problems, however, in handling liturgy as if it were statute law. The search is on for 'lighter' ways of authorizing less controversial and less central material.[1]

Promise, like its companion volume *Lent, Holy Week, Easter,* is 'commended by the House of Bishops'. In law this is little more than an expression of opinion informing the discretion that individual bishops and clergy already have under Canons B4 and B5. The discretion exists primarily for occasions for which Parliament or Synod make no provision. This rigidity is being eroded by increasing appeals to Canon B5.1 which gives the minister discretion to make variations 'which are not of substantial importance'.[2] The appellate role of the bishop in Canon B5 becomes the basis for episcopal commendation.

With *Promise,* reliance on 'commendation' and on Canon B5.1 began to run into trouble. The House of Bishops' minute of the commendation of *Promise* includes these words: 'The amendments made also enabled the Legal Advisor to advise that the Report, as amended, was in a form which could be commended for use by the House'. Comparison with the GS907 shows a number of significant revisions: an absolution for All Saints is replaced by the ASB form; alternative eucharistic prefaces have been made into proper prefaces[3]; new texts for an Epiphanytide baptism (GS907 pp.193-202) are omitted; a number of rubrics are carefully altered to leave the ASB order intact, e.g. the Service of Light 'precedes' (*Promise*) rather than 'forms the introduction to' (GS907 p.7) Evening Prayer; etc.

The most serious change from GS907 was the relegation of the Calendar and Lectionary material ('the framework within which the services are to be understood') to an Appendix with a warning that they require full synodical authorization and are not authorized for use. (There is some mystery as to why the alternative lectionary in *Lent, Holy Week, Easter* either escaped this treatment or did not provide a sufficient precedent for *Promise* to do so!).

---

[1] See, e.g. *The Worship of the Church as it approaches the Third Millennium* (GSMisc 364 published 30 April 1991) §66-72.

[2] e.g. variations from the ASB commended in *Lent, Holy Week, Easter* (1986); *The Collects for use with Rite B* (1987)—'the adaptation to the "thou" form, the use of BCP Collects and the "inclusive" language all come easily within the discretion canonically allowed'; Series 1 usages and customary variations from the BCP—countenanced in the House of Bishops' Minutes of 26 January 1988; *Making Women Visible* (1988—where only changing 'made man' in the Nicene Creed was explicitly ruled out by the Bishops—p.vi and §16.)

[3] Two alternative prefaces survive by being moved to non-eucharistic contexts (GS907 p232/3 to *Promise* V.D.5(3)a and b pp.251-3). Longer prefaces can lawfully be used with less awkwardness with Rite A's Second Eucharistic Prayer.

Understanding *Promise*

1. . . . the ethos of the season

Through the centuries Christian celebration of Christ's coming has taken place at many cultural levels. It has built on the inventions of popular culture, secular and religious, as well as theological reflection from some of the most creative periods in Christian history. These have included medieval meditation on death and judgment as well as fourth century exploration of the incarnation. (The Oxford movement drew on this last in re-introducing wonder at the incarnation into popular piety). All these and more find their place in *Promise;* it moves from austere meditation on judgment to simple forms of domestic celebration.

This richness means it is not possible to appeal to a simple, ancient 'authentic' tradition. The innovations of one era are the traditions of the next:

'Unlike the Easter cycle, this "Winter season" does not have a single liturgical shape which emerged fairly uniformly in the early centuries, and which the mainstream churches have retained . . . History does not finally settle even such questions as the relationship between Christmas and Epiphany, let alone the length and significance of Advent. If the past is a bit of a mess, then we do it (and ourselves) a disservice if we expect the present to be uniformly neat and predictable.' (Preface p.3).

2. . . . a resource book

Although *Promise* includes a complete rite for most major services, it is designed for thoughtful and selective use: 'there are many instances where worship will be more effective if the material is pondered carefully and then adapted to local use' (Preface). If all its richness were inflicted on one congregation they would be struggling with nausea and double vision. Apart from use in informal groups and at special services, much of its material can be used within the ordinary services of the ASB. Where a text involves a variable congregational part it can be printed on the notice sheet for the day. (Why is 'confession number 4' more threatening than 'song number 97'?!)

This more flexible approach is likely further to undermine a common Anglican distinction between liturgical texts (authorization required) and hymns or songs (anything goes). (Note the recommendation of the readings in *Carols for Today* by Michael Perry (p.39—after I.C.17).) The implications of this flexibility for unity and doctrine in the Church of England will need to be faced.

3. . . . the Service of Light

'Underlying the whole scheme is the Service of Light' (Preface). This is explained carefully, with a range of possible prayers and songs on pages 43-46, 338-9. It is not a 'catholic' invention nor does it require 'gothic' style. Christians from earliest times have seen light for the hours of darkness as a gift to be welcomed and as a symbol of Christ. In many different contexts lighting a candle can focus evening prayer. The key is to start simply and to remember that the songs and prayers are fundamentally about welcome. Michael Perry's *Psalms for Today* includes three versions of the ancient Christian hymn traditionally sung at this point.

The 'Acclamations of Light' (section 4) follow the style of traditional Jewish blessings. (h) and (i) vary the common ascription 'king of the universe'—which was probably introduced as a protest against imperial pretensions—and also explore feminine biblical imagery.

4. . . . conflict with the ASB

While most of *Promise* is about the enrichment of worship, it includes criticism of the Calendar and Lectionary of the ASB.[1] This conflict will be discussed in chapter 2; some resolution will be needed in thinking about worship after 2000.

5. . . . the impact of new thinking

The ASB was strongly influenced by a desire for simplicity, by the need for unity, and by Vatican II's single-minded concentration on 'the Paschal Mystery', the death and resurrection of Christ.

At a number of points the impact of new thinking and perspectives can be found in *Promise.* This is not simply a matter of scholarly publication; Portsmouth Cathedral, and even the Ambrosian rite from Milan, have left their mark. The 'Historical Commentary' (p.413-5) summarizes recent scholarship on the Calendar. The recovery in Epiphany of the scriptural link between revelation, the Baptism of Christ, the kingdom and mission owes much to the Orthodox. Kenneth Stevenson's scholarship has brought a new appreciation of Candlemas.[2] Some of the thinking behind Lectionary 2 with its undermining of the idea of a single Common Lectionary and its provision of more local discernment in the choice of readings, can be found in my *Reading the Bible at the Eucharist.*[3]

Using *Promise*

Three examples will illustrate different ways in which *Promise* could be used.

1. A church adopts the new approach to the winter calendar to allow a full exploration of the rich themes of the seasons before and after Christmas. Candlemas is used to mark the transition from the Christmas to the Easter cycle.

2. A church decides to make more of the popular, pastoral and mission emphases. The All Saints and All Souls material is linked to the pastoral care of the bereaved. Much is made of the Christingle Service and of New Year. Advent and Epiphany are low-key. There is a December vigil for prisoners and a lively service of readings in January to celebrate the theme of mission.

3. A church runs an autumn programme using Lectionary 2 modules on Jacob and Amos that continues through to Advent 2. The only Advent material used before that is a mid-week evening meditation on the Four Last Things. A parish kit for celebrating Advent at home is taken up by many families. The Epiphany Service for the Baptism of the Lord is used as a dramatic all-age service.

[1] See Introductory Outline (p.5) and the Introduction to Advent (p.91).
[2] 'The Origins and Development of Candlemas: A Struggle for Identity and Coherence' in J. Neil (ed.) *Time and Community* (Alexander, Washington, 1990).
[3] (Grove Worship Series no. 94, Grove Books, Bramcote, 1986).

2. WORD IN SEASON
by Michael Vasey

Hearing the scriptures

'Blessed Lord, who has caused all holy Scriptures to be written for our learning; Grant that we may in such wise hear them, read, mark, learn and inwardly digest them . . .' Cranmer's well-loved collect of Advent 2 assumes that the people of God's primary encounter with scripture will be by hearing. 'Read' in the collect has the archaic sense of 'study' as in 'I read chemistry at university'. The advent of cheap printing has alienated much of the modern world from public reading.

The scriptures took shape in a world in which public reading was an important part of community life; their content and style is coloured by this expectation. Thus St. Paul expected his letter to be read aloud to cummunities (cf. 1 Thess. 5.27, 2 Thess. 3.14, Col. 4.16, 2 Cor. 10.10, 11); even the letters written to individuals assume that others will hear them read. Listening together to the scriptures takes seriously the character of scripture and the corporate nature of the Christian life.

In the ancient church meeting to hear the scriptures was an important feature of church life. Justin describes the Sunday assembly as beginning with scripture reading 'for as long as time allows'. Evening meetings to listen to scripture—often before Sundays or other important days—were a major ingredient of church life. Often called 'vigils', they consisted of a rhythm of reading and response. The form of response would vary and might include silence, prayer, a song, a repeated refrain.

Many English Christians are familiar with only two examples of this sort of responsive listening to scripture. The first is in forms of the Office derived from Cranmer's Morning and Evening Prayer, in which Cranmer limited the readings to two—one from each Testament. The second is in Christmas Carol Services. This may give the impression that only a solemn or cathedral style is appropriate. In fact a wide variety of styles is possible and can help groups and individuals to appropriate and feed on scripture. Such prepared meditative reading can provide an important corrective to endless analytical dissection of scripture. All that is needed is imagination and a bit of planning!

The Promise of His Glory seeks to restore public reading of scripture and particularly this ancient pattern of reading and response. Chapter I.C. includes 17 different outlines for such corporate meditative reading. Many trace a theme through scripture finishing dramatically with a Gospel reading to proclaim Christ as the one to whom all scripture points (cf. Luke 24.27). Some work methodically through part of a particular book. The themes of these 'Patterns for Readings' pick up traditional theological themes of this part o f the year; others look out to the modern world, either in its suffering (2 'For Prisoners') or in mission (13, 14).

Much of the material in chapters I, VII and VIII is designed to enrich this responsive reading of scripture. (Note, for example, a number of 'laments' to be found in chapter VII.) In a modern context it is, of course, also possible to follow a reading with taped music or an appropriate slide.

All Saints to Candlemas

St. Paul's injunction to 'attend to the public reading of scripture' (1 Tim. 4.13) points to one way in which Christians are to get into the Bible. His encouragement 'let the word of Christ dwell in you richly as you teach and admonish . . . sing psalms, hymns and spiritual songs' (Col. 3.16) points to another. From early times Christians have met together for festival celebrations to enter into some aspect of Christ. For example the beautiful festival of Candlemas explores the moving story of Luke 2.22-38. St. Paul himself continued to note—and presumably to keep in a Christian way—the Jewish feasts of Possover and Pentecost (cf. 1 Cor. 5.7, 16.8).

Promise proposes an outline calendrical scheme which seeks to build on the major Christian festivals of this period and draw them into some type of integrated whole. It is set out clearly in the Introductory Outline (p.5) and in the Introductions to chapters II to VI. It moves through All Saints' Tide; A Season 'of the Kingdom'; Advent; Christmastide; Ephipanytide; and finally Candlemas (2 February), which marks the turning point from the Christmas 'cycle' to the run-up to Easter.

A number of features of this scheme are worth highlighting. It uses the period beginning with All Saints Day—the gloomy month of November—to explore the themes of heaven and death. It handles the popular anticipation of Christmas by giving an Advent feel to the two Sundays before Advent—following a hint in BCP and the practice of the Ambrosian Rite—and then allows a more Christmas feel to take over on Advent 3. It treats Ephiphany not just as an isolated feast but as the beginning of a short season of its own.

Lectionary 1 (pp.350-403) is intended to give effect to this calendrical scheme. It includes the three year lectionary of the Roman Catholic Church but is designed to allow other passages—initially assigned to morning or evening prayer—to be fed into the Sunday eucharist where this is desired. Starting with the third (or second) Sunday in Advent these include readings through appropriate prophetic and apocalyptic passages including Revelation. There is provision for readings from 1 Maccabees 1-4 to resonate with the Jewish festival of Hannukah.[1] The lectionary breaks new ground in the greater discretion it allows (see notes 5-8).

A new direction?

In some important respects these proposals in *Promise* run counter to the calendar and lectionary of the ASB, itself an adaptation of the 1967 Joint Liturgical Group lectionary.[2] In the nine Sundays before Christmas

---

[1] On the use of the Apocrypha see note 12 (p.376). Since the Reformation the Church of England has occasionally appointed readings from the Apocrypha without implying that they have the inspiration or authority of canonical scripture. *Promise* preserves the modern practice of always providing a canonical alternative. On the significance of these writings see R. T. Beckwith *Themelios* 1990 *15.3* pp.77-81. Note his comment, '1 Maccabees is not just good history but a narrative of heroic faith which has few equals'.

[2] For a detailed discussion of these lectionaries and their underlying principles see Michael Vasey *Reading the Bible at the Eucharist* (Grove Books, 1986). In one respect the situation has changed with the publication by JLG in 1990 of *A Four Year Lectionary* (JLG2) which adopts many of the strengths of the Roman Catholic lectionary and avoids explicit 'themes' but keeps the Trinitarian framework of JLG1.

the ASB unfolds the Old Testament story from Creation to the birth of Christ. A significant speech by Jean Mayland in the July 1990 General Synod debate on *Promise* strongly criticized the *Promise* scheme for undermining preaching on Creation and on the Old Testament in its natural, as opposed to typological, sense.

Disagreement about the JLG approach to Advent is not new[1]; also churches find it difficult to sustain its flow without interruption. The way forward is often spoken of in terms of a straight competition between JLG and the three year Roman Catholic lectionary. *Promise* provides a framework for a different response:

1. It proposes that the whole church should follow set thematic readings appropriate to the season for a 'closed period' from Advent 3 to Epiphany 1.

2. Outside this period it provides through Lectionaries 1 and 2 for readings to be varied locally so that different biblical books can be read on a semi-continuous basis. Lectionary 2 provides a series of undated lectionary modules for use in the 'open' season.

3. It recognizes that there is no absolutely fixed length for Advent: 'The preferred length of a season is partly determined by social factors.' (Enthusiasm for its own thematic calendrical scheme may obscure this recognition[2]!)

4. The ASB's unfolding of the Old Testament story would remain as one option in the period before Advent 3. Lectionary 2 provides other options—including ones that allow more Old Testament narrative to be read and take note of some of the important women in the biblical stories.

5. *Promise* parallels the ASB in allowing Creation to be the focus on the last Sunday in October if this is kept as Sunday in One World Week. It could be argued that the public reading of the early chapters of Genesis is too important to be left to whim. (In the BCP it was located from Septuagesima, a relic of the run up to Easter.) Would *Promise* have looked different if it had begun the autumn with Harvest?

6. If the lectionary proposals in *Promise* were authorized, Lectionary 2, notes 9 and 10, would provide authority for churches to design, within certain guidelines, their own reading schemes in the 'open season'. This would permit the practice behind the 'sermon series' of many evangelical churches. It would also provide some criteria as to whether the selection and presentation of scripture in such churches is different or responsible.

---

[1] Compare the criticisms in *Promise* (p.92 and elsewhere) with Peter Cobb in *The Study of Liturgy* (SPCK, 1978) pp.417-18. JLG is defended, for example, by Richard Buxton in 'Advent' in J. G. Davies (ed.) *A New Dictionary of Liturgy and Worship* (SCM, 1986). An interesting middle way was proposed by Tony Gelston in 'The Future of Advent' in *Scripture Bulletin* vol. 18.1 1987.
[2] *Promise* pp.6-7.

3. CHRISTMAS:
FOLK FESTIVAL OR FEAST OF THE INCARNATION?

by Trevor Lloyd

1. Christmas comes but ...

At the heart of the season covered by this book is the festival of the incarnation. In theory, Advent prepares for it and Epiphany to Candlemas continues and reinforces the theme. Those responsible for worship in the local church would do well to examine and discuss the meaning and intention of the celebration of Christmas. What kind of festival is it? What is it that we wish to celebrate (and is it possible that there might be a slightly different answer to this from one year to the next)? Are we falling into the danger of inventing and arranging more occasions on which the incarnation, in one form or other, is the main theme, simply because commercial pressures prevent us from doing that at Christmas itself? How does the 'weight' given to the incarnation compare with the amount of time and energy we spend as a church celebrating the crucifixion and resurrection?

Christmas as folk festival

It may help such a discussion to outline some different ways of looking at Christmas. Christmas may be seen as a folk festival, reinforcing 'Christian' values. For many people, celebrating the Christmas events, at home, on TV or at church, brings with it the simple assurance that God is still around and of some importance. Re-telling the old Christmas story, in school nativities or in carol services, makes him somehow more present. Others would see the value of Christmas in re-assuring us that the old values are still there somewhere in the background. These are values such as

—the importance of children. Christmas is 'the children's festival', symbolized by the baby in the crib. It may be easier to relate to a God who is vulnerable, or spoken of in language recognized from childhood.

—the place of the family in society. This concept may not be at all related to the holy family, honoured at any other time of year, but its importance at Christmas is seen in such things as the distances travelled by many to be home with their extended families, or by the hallowed position of the family dinner on Christmas Day.

—giving and receiving. Gifts seem to have always had a place at the centre of the Christmas story. The gold, frankincense and myrrh are clear obstacles to any attempt to separate the story of the wise men from the nativity narratives ... Putting the wise men alongside the shepherds ensures a biblical warrant for the Christmas gifts.[1]

—caring. Christmas is seen as a time to care for others, to appeal for money for charity, to think about prisoners, refugees, the homeless. Caring agencies probably rightly stir up a large amount of generosity, perhaps partly generated by guilt at what is spent on celebrating Christmas. And even before caring agencies there were Scrooge and good King Wenceslaus ...

[1] A good calendrical case can be made for this, based on the fact that in the Eastern Church 6 January is the festival of the incarnation, with these themes present together.

These values which affect our behaviour today are 'old' values, and gain in impact by being placed in a nostalgic setting. For many, Christmas, often isolated from the normal place of work or living, is a time for escapism and nostalgia. Much of our current image of Christmas is straight out of Dickens, reflected and recreated in cards, films and songs. Nineteenth century costume, top hats, stage coaches, holly and mistletoe all unite to reinforce the romantic image. The church's worship is a necessary part of the image, maintaining the romantic view and its values. Threaten to change the church's contribution, or remove it, and you threaten the image and its values as well.

Christmas as national celebration

This is really another, but particularly English, part of the 'folk' view of Christmas. Christmas gives the nation a sense of unity, perhaps symbolized by the monarch's Christmas broadcast, but also evidenced in such things as large numbers of people off work at the same time, parties at work and home, crowds of shoppers, the volume of postal traffic as people keep in touch. This sense of everyone being involved in one overriding event is no doubt good for the sense of nationhood. People of other faiths find it possible to join in much of the Christmas celebration, including nativity plays and carol concerts: should this make the church water down words about the divinity or virgin birth of Jesus, or take sensitively the opportunities for friendship and evangelism?

Christmas as commercial bonanza

A glance at the pop charts, TV ads for Harvey's Bristol Cream, bulging toy shops, will show how the English Christmas is put to good commercial use. Christmas as a commercial bonanza is a fact of life, effectively extending the Christmas season from September to Christmas Eve (when the church's Christmas season officially begins!).

Christmas as a revolutionary event

There are those, both Christian and non-Christian, who view the modern keeping of Christmas with revulsion, and opt out of most of these activities. 'Secular' caring agencies as well as Christian ones give Christmas Day to providing food for those in need; Oxfam fills people with shame at the amount on the Christmas dinner plate; and attention is focussed on the messiness and poverty of the incarnation, and the refugee status of the holy family. Even the nostalgics have their problems. As with memories of white Christmasses, this particular Christmas is never as good as Christmas used to be: this means that people are frequently coping with unreal expectations, failure to fulfil them, and consequent depression, every Christmas. Some of this is captured in the liturgy (for example the confession in the Crib Service (pp.165-6) or the intercessions (p.169). But it is all fairly gentle. Contrast the Preface of the Holy Innocents (p.199), which says they 'died cruelly, not yet knowing the new-born Christ, that your grace might be made perfect in human weakness . . .' with the emotion and earthiness of the prayer for the same day in the New Zealand liturgy:

'Loving Jesus, let the tears of Rachel express our desolation, let her weep for battered babies and clinical deformity.'[1]

[1] See note at foot of p.12 overleaf.

Christmas for the local church

Those who plan and lead the local church's worship should be encouraged to do some missionary and incarnational theology, in planning for the Christmas season. Should the church, in order to proclaim and celebrate the incarnation, stand out against the folk, national, commercial and revolutionary pressures of society? This is the more rigorist position, largely adopted by *Promise* and reflecting the 'otherness' of the faith. But it could be argued that a more truly incarnational position for the church, reflecting the way in which the Saviour came to earth, would be not collusion, but a deep immersion in the messiness of commerce, revolution and folk half-truths. This is the mission dilemma which the church faces continually, not just at Christmas. Each local church will come to its own conclusion. But this glance at the society in which we celebrate Christmas indicates some areas in which liturgy and mission come together. How can we best market (note the commercial implications!) and construct the services which large numbers of those with little or no faith attend, in such a way as to proclaim the gospel and involve them in the life of the Christian community? Examine one by one services such as the Carol Service, Christingle, Toy Service or Crib Blessing, Family Service—and even Midnight Communion. How can the nostalgia and folk expectations be partly met (it is bad marketing to tell people that what they think they want is not on offer), while also meeting the unexpressed longing for some personal reassurance that God is still around? Is there warmth and familiarity—warmth of welcome as well as a good heating system, and some familiar carols and readings and other worship texts? Do the visual images, teaching aids, choreography of movements, colour and freshness of robes and decorations, and the clarity with which the message is spelt out stand up to the competition in the market place of the TV and the stores?

In all this *Promise* does not take one particular line or offer an exclusive package. But church leaders who are working their way through issues such as these will find in *Promise* an excellent mine of structures and resources which will enable them to celebrate Christmas in a way that is right for their community, this year. We will briefly look at each section in turn.

2. The Carol Service

One of the advantages of the Service of Light noted earlier is that it can provide a structure—which will gradually become familiar—for services of bible reading, music and meditation at different points in the calendar. Another advantage is that it provides specifically for thanksgivings, and those suggested, for Christmas and for the Blessed Virgin Mary, are full of good incarnational theology expressed in strong visual images ('and dwelt in the darkness of her womb,') even if occasionally it might set the mind searching for the source of the allusion ('in her your glory shines as in the burning bush.' 1 B (4)j, p.13).

[1] New Zealand Prayer Book (Collins, 1989) p.678. The calendar itself might help in some of the mass. That 'empty' period after Christmas Day, created partly by the heavy commercial build-up to Christmas with its over-emphasis on families, frequently results in marriage breakdowns and the suicide of single people in bedsits. But is it sufficient simply to make a fuller and better provision for the Christmas Saints, as *Promise* does, without suggesting how such people might be encouraged to come, in the days after Christmas, when the tradition in many places (among clergy as well) is to opt out?

12

To make full use of this link with the resources in the Service of Light it is essential to have that chapter open at the same time: that is where the suggested five different patterns of Carol Service readings are to be found. One of these is the traditional King's College pattern, and Eric Milner-White's famous bidding prayer is to be found both here in the Carol Service section (with a few informative lines of history) and also in the Service of Light (where it is accompanied by the traditional collect and blessing). Though a modern equivalent bidding is provided (p.149), there is still a need for a warmer and richer bidding or introduction to the intention of the service; but the Commission are probably right not to provide this, as the language will need to reflect local experience and expectations, and vary from year to year.

Each of the other patterns of readings respects the integrity of one of the Gospels. One (1.C.7) is a sequence in seven sections of Luke's birth narrative, with alternatives suggested in case some parts are used as canticles. One (1.C.9) is Johannine, in taking the theme of the new creation through four Old Testament readings from Genesis, Proverbs and Isaiah, to Hebrews 1 and Revelation 22 in the New Testament, climaxing in the only reading from John in the traditional Gospel, John 1.1-14. Those from Matthew and Luke are similar to this in their thematic approach, the first tracing the theme of the King and his Kingdom (much better as an Advent set) and the second giving us some rich selections on Good News for the Poor. The main problem about these last three sets of readings is that while they do a good job in tracing (and providing psalms for meditation on) the development of the theological concepts that paved the way for the recognition of Jesus as Son of God, King and Messiah, they do not actually tell the Christmas story in the way many Carol Service attenders will expect to hear. This may be very good for some congregations, particularly where this occasion is celebrated largely by the usual church attenders who need the stimulation to think more deeply about the meaning behind the story they already know. But there will be other congregations where, if they are not to have the King's pattern or the Luke narrative every year, the leaders will take the hint at the end of this section (p.151) and 'contrive' other patterns. A note at the end of the sets of readings in 'The Service of Light' may guide them to Carols for Today (ed. Michael Perry, Hodder 1986), where five more sets are provided, some for two readers or arranged in parts, and all with a helpful one-line introduction which traces the development of the story. But for some people those sets will seem an unhelpful jumble as they mix readings from the different Gospels, and they will find the only solution is to construct their own set of readings: fruitful Advent preparation for a bible study or theological discussion group!

This brings us back to the Commission's own intentions, expressed in the introduction (p.145): 'Here we have not given one form, but provided rich resources . . . this material will enable them to devise something tailored to their needs and opportunities.' Those who plan worship need their imaginations stimulated to make use of the flexibility of the Carol Service pattern to explore that relationship between the conservative demands of the folk occasion and the radical opportunities for stirring the social conscience and facing people with the demands of the gospel. Stories of what others have done are easily exchanged. As long ago as 1978 the Fisher-folk produced a Christmas kit with drama, mime, songs on tape, suggestions for graphic arts, dance and how to develop service outlines, with ideas on involving the whole congregation. School nativity plays or TV presentations sometimes provide ideas on how to link the historic bible story with the present, using a chief story-teller (the 'president') to hold the story together, using interviews and visuals, musical backing as well as the usual rich variety of solo and choral music. Are the traditional beginnings and endings always necessary? I have seen a Carol Service begin with a group of singers in outdoor clothes, with a lantern, singing as the congregation arrive, developing later into a choir . . . and I have seen it end with mince pies and coffee as an essential part of celebrating the incarnation, in a village church so tightly packed that no one could leave anyway!

The Christingle Service

This is one of three services the Commission have produced for the Christmas season with families and children especially in mind: the other two are the Crib Service and a Family Service. The first Christingle took place in Wetteravia on 24 December 1747, when Bishop de Watteville distributed lighted candles to the children, with a red ribbon symbolizing the blood of Christ. The symbol is a powerful one, and the Commission has followed the Moravian custom of not accompanying such obvious symbolism with any explanatory formula at the point at which it happens. In England the service is closely associated with the giving of money to The Children's Society, 'who introduced it into the Anglican Church in 1968'.[1] It is possible to trace the modern shape of the Christingle, with the orange representing the world, the candle the Light of the World, the red ribbon his blood shed for the world, the white frill purity, and the sweets or nuts the fruit of the earth, back to the middle of the last century in England. In those days it was made in the home, for use in the home, and it is a pity that this link between home and church is not brought out by the Commission, either in the preparation of the Christingles, or, more importantly, in what might be made of the idea of the light of Christ for the world being carried out of church and continuing to shine at home, perhaps in the window as a symbol of that light in our street.

The structure of the service in *Promise* is different from that publicized by The Children's Society. There is a richer provision of texts, with a suggested introductory bidding (based on David Silk and Taizé), an option of two thanksgivings, one of which is a responsive one closely based on John 1, and the possibility of a fuller ministry or the word. Because of this (as well as the mechanics of the service), those planning the worship will need to ensure that the service does not get too long for the children. Another factor is that the service moves to a climax, provided the later position for distributing the Christingles (at section 11) is used. This involves putting the prayers (whether for The Children's Society or not) after the ministry of the word, in a pattern familiar from the eucharist, rather than at the end,

[1] Children's Society Information Pack.

after the distribution. But the most obvious change in structure is that the offering of money is separated from the distribution of the Christingles. This is because the Commission felt very strongly that the wrong theological message was being given in a symbolic action where 'children present gift envelopes containing money . . . receiving in return their Christingles' (as the Children's Society Information Pack puts it). So the exchange of cash for the symbol of Christ has gone (it does in any case take pretty slick handling to get the money off the children before they have their hands full of orange and sweets!), with the receiving in open hands of the symbol as the climax to the service, and the collection after the talk and before the prayers. And there is no reason why the offerings on this occasion should not be presented by a group of children.

The climax is heightened by the use of some good acclamations, both at the distribution and at the dismissal: they work well if shouted. Some thought needs to be given to the possibilities and dangers of the end of the service. Processing round the inside of the church, forming a circle or a cross for the last part of the worship, can be very effective. So too can dance, by a small and disciplined group of adults or older children. But there should be warnings about the danger of moving with lighted candles, and an instruction to blow the candles out all at once rather than in uncertain and haphazard fashion. This section ends with suggested readings and hymns, including an excellent new Christingle hymn written in 1988 by Bishop Timothy Dudley-Smith.

3. A Crib Service
This is intended to provide something for Christmas Eve which is non-sacramental and suitable either for children or for an adult vigil. Certainly the need for the former is obvious, with many churches packed on Christmas Eve for a service for children, whether it is a family service, toy service or blessing of the crib. In some places it is popular because it gets the children out of the way while the massive Christmas feeding preparations continue; in others, it is an oasis of spiritual refreshment for the whole family in the middle of the secular stress. For some—and this is a point to be watched—it has come to replace going to church on Christmas Day ('when we are too busy').

The Commission are openly tentative in presenting this service: 'some of the following material may be useful' . . . 'whatever structure is adopted . . .'. And this is right and helpful, providing a structure while encouraging the local church to design one to fit its own circumstances.

The structure provided is a helpful one on which to base an informal family service, though those leading it may well wish to provide less formal words, for example for the Introduction. The opening greeting could be used as an acclamation to punctuate the service as it moves from one section to the next. The opening rite, predictably, is an optional candle-lighting ceremony. Those planning the pattern of Christmas season services should make sure that candle-lighting does not occur on every occasion otherwise the symbol loses its impact! The confession follows a helpful story pattern, with one or two lines from the Christmas story, a relevant request for forgiveness, and a responsive acknowledgement of sin and prayer for forgiveness. Some may wish to omit the Psalm which follows, or to replace it with another portion of praise. It is important that this does not become more important than the helpful longer thanksgiving, with its climactic repeated acclamations, which follows the ministry of the word. It is perhaps surprising, in the family service context, that there is no explicit provision for a talk. This may easily be inserted into Section 6 (the Service of the Word) and would be regarded by many as essential if this service is to fulfil the function of taking a folk-centred view of Christmas and using it evangelistically. Even in the case of an adult vigil, with a series of readings, canticles and collects (as provided in the sets of readings from Chapter 1, the Service of Light, discussed above under Carol Services). There might still be a need for an occasional word of interpretation or a guide to the theme of meditation.

While for many evangelicals the central visual aspect of the service might be the visual aid used in the talk, for others the central feature will be the procession to the Christmas crib. Evangelicals are generally not very good at stage-managing processions, or marching around with crib figures. It might perhaps be helpful to suggest various different ways of doing this, as part of the thanksgiving. Thought should be given to the position of the crib, preferably *not* in the centre at the front of the church. It also needs to be of sufficient size to be visible as a focus in this part of the service. This would also ensure that the figures, if they are to be carried, are sufficiently large. In some places, the crib is completely set up, apart from the figure of the Christ child, and this is carried, held high, in solemn procession during the thanksgiving. In other places, the crib may be built up, with figures added at different stages during the telling of the story in the ministry of the word. There is no need for the figures to be carried in solemn procession: they could be brought forward by children. Nor are three-dimensional figures essential. It may be easier to use two-dimensional cardboard cutouts to get the size big enough to be seen. All the children in the church might gather informally around the crib, or there might be some kind of procession, though care should be taken to ensure that this is not too solemn and also to avoid any impression of worship being focussed on the symbolic figures themselves. This is, as the Commission's introduction says, basically a teaching service with the figures used in that context.

Again, the more adventurous liturgical parishes may wish to emphasize the link between home and church by encouraging the building of a Christmas crib at home, with the gradual addition of figures, perhaps accompanied by suitable versicles and responses, acclamation, a prayer or a chorus sung by the whole family.

More material on the crib can be found in Section E1 (Prayers at the Christmas Crib, p.190f.). Here there are helpful suggestions about the building of the crib and the teaching opportunity it provides at an earlier stage than Christmas Eve. The possibility of using the whole church as a route towards the Christmas crib, with figures such as the wise men en route in a different part of the church, is an interesting one. There is also a helpful discussion about the time at which the crib ought to be moved. In practice, this should depend on the particular theological pattern being followed by the church in this particular year.

It is in this section that the use of the crib 'as a personal means of devotion outside the liturgy' appears, as opposed to the teaching emphasis in the crib service. There is no explicit discussion—and such a service book is not the place for it—of how something physical and symbolic such as the crib with its figures might be used as a personal means of devotion and there may be some who would wish to question this in the light of the mediaeval abuse of such representative figures. There is scope for more serious work to be done from the evangelical tradition on the whole area of icons, stained glass, statues etc.

In the Roman Catholic Church, there is no official rite for the blessing of the crib, though it always occurs, as suggested here in the Order for the Eucharist of Christmas Night or Morning (p.171) as a preliminary rite at the start of Mass. The whole concept of blesing is another area on which more work needs to be done. It might have been hoped that this would be stimulated by the publication of the ICEL *Draft Book of Blessings*.[1] Though there is no provision for blessing the crib, the normal pattern of provision, after an introduction putting the blessing into the pastoral context, is to provide an introductory rite, including a paragraph about the intention for the use of the object, several selections of scripture, intercessions for the use of the object and a prayer of blessing which is normally a blessing of God ('Blessed are you, Lord our God . . .') followed by a prayer for those who are going to use the object. Evangelicals would almost certainly find this Roman pattern preferable to that in *Promise* where the request to God 'Bless this crib' is followed by a mediaeval form 'We hallow this crib of Christmas'. This form should certainly stimulate discussion on what the expected result of the prayer might be. The rest of this section has some helpful prayers focussing on the different figures around the crib, and their spiritual implications for us.

4. A Service for Christmas Morning

This is the third family-oriented service, and provides a pattern which might be used either on Christmas morning, or, with suitable amendments, at some earlier stage. Again, there is an indication that other structures might be adopted, and direction to other parts of the book where there is useful material. The service moves from the opening acclamations and greeting, through a kyrie penitential section to the ministry of the word, thanksgiving and prayers of intercession based on Isaiah 9.6. Some might be a little hesitant about using the new translation of the Christological section of the Athanasian Creed from 'Patterns', but this may easily be replaced by something more acceptable to children.

5. Eucharist of Christmas Night or Morning

This is, as the introduction states, 'the heart of the Christmas celebration of the incarnation' (p.145), and is so designed that it will fit either a midnight or a morning celebration. The introductory rite is centred round the crib, and though the blessing of the crib (Section 2) is optional, the

[1] The green book draft of *The Book of Blessings* was published in 1987 by the International Commission on English in the Liturgy and contains a very helpful theological and historical introduction as well as over 500 pages of Blessings.

ministers (Section 1) go to the crib, and it is the place from which the prayers of penitence are led.[1] There are many churches which will not have a crib, and if they had might not wish to use it as the focus of the Liturgy.

The opening greeting is deliberately paradoxical, capturing the mystery, wonder and glory of this night. Some might find it too precious, or prefer the more traditional way a sentence of scripture. The confession is the one from *Patterns* which has also been used in the Crib Service, but with the ASB absolution (for legal reasons)[2] replacing the richer form in the draft service, 'May the God of all healing and forgiveness draw you to himself, that you may behold the glory of his Son, the Word made flesh, and be cleansed from all your sins through . . .'.

The movement of the ministers from the crib to wherever the Ministry of the Word happens may be covered by the Gloria in Excelsis or a hymn, and it is only after this that the president greets the people. For some, this may seem a little late in the day (or night), but it does solemnly mark the beginning of the congregations's serious look at the Word of God. Here an Old Testament canticle is provided, as well as a Gospel acclamation. This works better as a response to the Gospel (as in the draft service) than as an introduction to it (its position here, with the option of having it afterwards as well). The intercession (again duplicated in *Patterns*) is responsive, recalling the events of the incarnation and relating them to contemporary needs. It feels better at night. The change in the words of the intercession from 'in this holy night' to 'on this holy day' gently raises the question, 'is the nature of the celebration at night different from that in the morning?' Does the night celebration take on something of the feeling of re-enactment (we are there with Mary and Joseph going through it with them), while the morning is a celebration—with relief and joy—of the momentous event that has taken place?

From the Peace (with its new introductory words) onwards all is fairly standard. One of the ASB Prefaces is included, with a new composition as an alternative. Alternative post-communion prayers are provided, for night and day, and there is one of the newly popular three-part solemn blessings.

At the end of this chapter there are proper prefaces and post-communion prayers for the post-Christmas saints, and some materials for New Year, with indications of other sections of the book where further resources might be found, such as the Service of Light. That service provides a good pattern for a Watch Night Service. While there is more provision here than in most Anglican prayer books, where the Naming of Jesus predominates as the theme, let there be good creative thinking in the parish about the purpose and the opportunities of such an occasion. How are ordinary pagan people thinking about this day? Are we providing a comfortable piece of folk liturgy, or harnessing their hopes and longings for the future and leading them in the direction of Christ? The local church will want to consider the amount of silence in the service, the use of solo, instrumental or recorded music, the possibility of using the occasion for re-commitment using some of the material in the Epiphany service (pp.220-1 Chapter V.C.26), and whether the service is a climax to a period of discussion, prayer and seeking God's will for the future. Much will depend on what creative use is made of these resources.

[1] The words in Section 3, 'are said at the crib' are more mandatory than the normal tentative style of the *Promise* rubrics.
[2] As with the confession and absolution, the lawyers have taken the fact that the ASB allows alternatives for confession and blessing to mean that any alternatives are permitted, while the absolution and dismissal, having only one form in the ASB, may not be changed.

4. ADVENT, EPIPHANY, AND
THE PRESENTATION OF CHRIST IN THE TEMPLE

by Jane Sinclair

ADVENT

If the celebration of the birth of Christ is the high point of the seasons covered by *The Promise of His Glory,* Advent, Epiphany and Candlemas provide the surrounding means of preparing for and reflecting on the views which that high point offers.

The provision for the weeks preceding Advent and for Advent itself, with its vigil and carol services, its penitential rites, and its resources for use in church and home are amongst the most distinctive in the book. The Liturgical Commission acknowledges and to a degree embraces the tensions between the popular anticipation of Christmas (with Father Christmas appearing in some shops before Guy Fawkes Day on 5 November!) and the sober celebration of Advent traditionally kept by the Church. The Commission speak of their hope 'to restore to the Church the distinctive eschatological thrust of Advent, with its expectant longing for the coming of Christ's kingdom in power and the spirit of penitence which that engenders' (p.91). Nonetheless, 'we need to use creatively the stubborn popular conception of Advent as a lead into the Christmas festival' (p.91).

The Shape of Advent

The four week Advent is retained in *The Promise of His Glory,* but encouragement is given to the local church to treat these four weeks with some flexibility, and possibly to extend them back through November towards All Saints' Day (November 1). With the imaginative use of the lectionary and calendrical provisions in *The Promise of His Glory* (at present unauthorized) a church may treat the themes of the coming Kingdom of Christ in more depth than is possible using the ASB or the Book of Common Prayer. The three Sundays following All Saints' Day are designated by the Commission 'Sundays of the Kingdom', and the readings suggested for these Sundays reflect Kingdom themes. These themes might be developed in Sunday worship with the greater use of penitential material (for example, from Section C of the Advent resources, pp.102-127; or from the ASB). Eschatological and penitential hymns and songs would be appropriate for these Sundays.[1]

Within Advent itself a change of gear is indicated on the two Sundays immediately preceding Christmas. At this point the whole church is encouraged to focus on John the Baptist and Mary, as the two immediate forerunners of the Incarnation itself. Between Advent 3 and Epiphany 1 it is strongly suggested that local church preferences should give way to the common celebration of the incarnation of Christ and his manifestation to the world.

[1] There are good examples given in the thematic indexes of M. Perry and D. Peacock (eds.) *Songs from the Psalms,* (Hodder & Stoughton); M. Perry and D. Iliff, (eds.) *Psalms for Today,* (Hodder & Stoughton); *Hymns and Songs of Fellowship* (Kingsway Publications); R. Fudge, P. Horrobin and G. Leavers (eds.) *Mission Praise I and II,* (Marshall Pickering); and M. Baughen (ed.) *Hymns for Today's Church,* (Hodder & Stoughton).

Advent vigil and carol services

Local churches may choose to make as much of traditional Advent themes as pastoral need requires. The growth of the Advent carol service is acknowledged in *The Promise of His Glory* with the suggestion that churches may like to adapt the Service of Light (chapter I, p.11) to an Advent theme. Beware the temptation to let the darkness/light theme predominate in Advent. It is easy to have Advent, Christmas, Epiphany and Candlemas celebrations all marked with candles and seeming to be much of a muchness.[1] The patterns of readings for an Advent vigil or carol service (chapter III B pp.95-101) suggest as alternative themes a 'vigil for prisoners', 'the forerunner' and 'good news for the poor', any of which would provide fruitful resources for churches in the decade of evangelism. The suggested bidding prayers are similar in form and content to the traditional Christmas carol service bidding prayers. If any of this material is to be used in all-age worship, it may be appropriate to adapt the language of the biddings and prayers accordingly. With imagination and good amplification it is possible to reduce the number of readings and give space for musical and prayer contributions from the congregation. It would also be worth mining the rich resources of missionary societies, and such groups as Amnesty International for other material if one of the alternative themes is to be used.

Penitential services

Two penitential rites are provided (chapter III, C, p.102) for use during Advent; Word services based on the traditional Four Last Things (death, judgment, heaven and hell), and on the traditional Advent Antiphons (the Great 'O's). It is suggested that either of these services might stand on its own as an evening vigil on one Sunday in Advent, or it might be combined with a service of Holy Communion (forming an extended ministry of the Word with penitence), or it might stand as a simple service of penitence, perhaps celebrated by an Advent study group at home, or at a mid-week church prayer meeting. The services are solemn in feel and are designed to enable the careful and prayerful reflection upon Scriptural themes which have often been marginalized in the church's regular worship. Traditional prayers and texts are suggested for use, with some alternative provision made for inclusive language (e.g. p.106). Either service might be treated as a quiet meditation, or as a livelier celebration of our hope in Christ. Much will depend upon the style and quality of the music that is chosen, and what, if any, visual focus is available for the service (a simple lectern with a Bible set in the midst of the people? A plain cross on the Holy Table? A banner with the words 'Lord have mercy' or 'Come, Lord Jesus!' hung on the wall? etc.).

Some of the suggested texts may be thought to be couched in rather archaic language for local congregations (notably the Dies Irae, p.121). Generally, alternatives to such texts are provided (see p.123 for alternatives paraphrases of the Dies Irae). It would also be in keeping with the tenor of these services to make use of some of the great traditional

---

[1] The use of candles in the seasons of Advent, Epiphany and Candlemas is possible on many occasions. Commonsense suggests that the group or person responsible for the planning of worship during these seasons will use candles judiciously and effectively, rather than adopt a 'candles with chips' approach to every major service!

Advent hymns of judgment and hope: 'Lo, he comes with clouds descending'; 'O come, O come, Immanuel'; 'Sleepers wake'; 'Come, thou long expected Jesus'.

The acts of penitence themselves in these services have a four-fold shape; (a) an examination of conscience, (b) a prayer for God's mercy, (c) a confession (often couched in the first person singular), and (d) a declaration of absolution. Various forms are given, with considerable freedom to the minister to lead (a) and (b) as she or he thinks most appropriate. Among the alternative forms of confession and absolution in appendix B (p.124f.) is one which allows for water to be prayed over and sprinkled on the congregation as a sign of absolution. In many churches, some teaching on the use of water in this way would need to form part of an address earlier in the service if this action were to be an edifying one. The use of water in this way is meant to stand as a reminder of our common baptism, and the forgiveness for our sins which is a benefit of that baptism into the death of Christ.

Advent resources for church and home

As well as some alternative material[1] for use in ASB-style services (invitations to confession, forms of penitence and intercession, introductions to the Peace, proper prefaces, post-communion prayers, and forms of blessing), chapter III, E, pp.136-144 provides suggestions for the use of an Advent Wreath, a Jesse Tree, Saturday evening prayers at home, and various Table prayers to be used at meals during the season.

The Advent Wreath is now commonly used in churches on the four Sundays preceding Christmas, and on Christmas Day itself. It is suggested that the use of such a wreath might be made an integral part of Sunday morning worship, with the appropriate candle(s) being lit either after the Gospel reading, or before the Peace, or after the distribution of communion, rather than simply 'got out of the way' before or during the first hymn. Suggested prayers are provided, including a shorter alternative one for each Sunday, suitable for an all-age congregation to pray together.

The transformation of the Victorian, not to say Teutonic, Christmas tree into a Jesse Tree (recalling, in symbols with which it is decorated, the history of our salvation) is explained on p.141. It is not difficult to imagine how these ideas might be adapted for use in the home when decorating the Christmas tree, and when praying at home prior to and during the Christmas season. These prayers may be linked very simply with those which might be said as a grace at evening meal times. Sunday lunches might also be marked by the use of an Advent wreath with prayers at home in addition to or instead of a wreath at church.

EPIPHANY

The feast of the Epiphany 'marks a new start after the Christmas break' (p.6) with its emphasis on the revelation of Christ to the world and the mission of the Church to proclaim the good news.

[1] Some of these resources have already been published in GS 898, *Patterns for Worship*, (CHP, 1989).

The shape of Epiphany
The lectionary and calendrical material in *The Promise of His Glory* suggest two possible ways of handling Epiphanytide. Lectionary 2 allows for a brief Epiphany season, consisting of Epiphany itself (6 January) and the Sunday following (Epiphany 1) marking the Feast of the Baptism of the Lord (see below for comment). Thereafter, the local church may opt to follow one of the lectionary modules of sequential Scriptural readings up to the beginning of Lent.

The main thrust the calendar in *The Promise of His Glory* (complemented by the provision of Lectionary 1) sees the season of the Epiphany as mirroring those of Advent and Easter. From Christmas/Epiphany to the feast of the Presentation of Christ in the Temple (2 February) is the season of the Incarnation. The Sundays between 6 January and 2 February are named as Sundays of Epiphany, rather than Sundays after Epiphany.

The feast of the Baptism of the Lord (Epiphany 1)
In the western church, the Epiphany has traditionally centred upon the visit of the magi to Bethlehem (Matt. 2.1ff.). However, a major service of Epiphanytide provided by the Commission (p.210) draws in addition on traditions which have featured more prominently within the celebrations of the eastern church: notably, the Baptism of Christ (Mark 1.9ff.) and the Johannine tradition of the revelation of Christ at Cana in Galilee (John 2.1ff.). The order of service commended by the house of Bishops differs significantly from that originally published in GS 907.[1] There is no provision in the commended service for the celebration of baptism itself during the rite.

The service is designed primarily as a service of the Word, for use on Epiphany 1, or at any other suitable time during Epiphanytide. It takes the form of a three-part procession with symbols (one or more of the gifts brought by the wise men; wine, and water), and culminates in the renewal of the Covenant by the congregation. Readings from Scripture and prayers intersperse the processions, and music may be played or sung as deemed appropriate. Notes are given[1] on how to adapt the service so that it may form part of a service of Holy Communion. It is most appropriate, in this case, to vary the order of the processions so that sections 10-14 ('The new creation is revealed in the water made wine') occur after the renewal of the Covenant and immediately prior to the preparation of the gifts for the Holy Communion.

The service may be celebrated with formality (president, deacon, robed choir, and anthems), or may very well be celebrated in a relaxed and informal manner (with children carrying the symbols to the appropriate part of the church, or to a crib outside? With banners being waved? And suitable songs played or sung etc.). The important thing is to allow the Scripture to be heard clearly (special amplification may be needed), and the symbols to be seen. Done boldly, this service can provide a rich means of enabling the people of God to celebrate the revelation of Christ with Word, bodies and buildings in harmony.

[1] GS 907, *The Promise of His Glory*, (CHP, 1990), pp. 193-202. The omission was made at the request of the House of Bishops. Questions about liturgical provision for Christian initiation presently rest with the House of Bishops.
[2] *The Promise of His Glory*, Chapter V. C, p.10, note 3.

The climax of the service is to be found in the Renewal of the Covenant (chapter V. C, sections 24-26, pp.218-221). This is preceded by a prayer made over the water which has been brought in procession and poured into the font or a suitable receptacle visible to the congregation (sections 21 and 22, pp.216-218). The first of these prayers (p.216) is modelled on a combination of the form of the prayer said over the water in the ASB Baptism service[1] ('bless this water, that . . .'), and an ASB Rite A Eucharistic Prayer[2] (use of Sursum Corda and preface-style material). It has an optional preface with a distinctively Byzantine feel.[3] The central petition itself is for the worshippers: that they may be renewed in the service of God.[4] The alternative to this prayer (section 22) is fully responsive in form. The epiclesis over the water is explicit[5], but the petition for the worshippers is again that they may be renewed in their service of Christ.

These prayers are, however, preliminary to the congregational Renewal of the Covenant which follows in two alternative forms. The first is more explicitly baptismal in feel, drawing on the Apostles' Creed and on an act of dedication in the service of Christ.[6] The alternative form is modelled closely on the Methodist Covenant service, which itself is often used at or around the New Year. Each act of dedication is weighty, and ought not to be sprung on an unprepared congregation. Ideally, the whole congregation will be invited to prepare beforehand to make this act of rededication (through work in Advent house groups, or perhaps with their family of friends in the period leading up to Epiphanytide).

The Promise of His Glory (chapter V. B and D) contains further rich resources of proper materials for use during Epiphanytide (vigils, service of light, carol services; greetings, acclamations, forms of intercession, introductions to the confession and to the peace, acts of thanksgiving, etc.). These latter are set out as for use in services of the Holy Communion, but much of this material could well be used in services of Morning or Evening Prayer, or in Sunday all-age worship. As in the main provision for Epiphany 1, rubrics on p.231 allow for water to be sprinkled on the congregation[7] at Holy Communion following an act of thanksgiving over water and corporate penitence. Treated boldly, with water distributed liberally, such sprinkling can provide an effective link between teaching about the baptism of Christ and his new creation, and our own baptism.

---

[1] For example, ASB, p 231.
[2] For example, ASB, p 130.
[3] A shortened version of this prayer is printed on p.232 of *The Promise of His Glory*.
[4] The phraseology assumes that all the worshippers present have already been baptized. The prayer is not intended by the Commission to raise any questions about the efficacy of the worshippers' baptism. The phrase 'that we . . . may be renewed in your image' is immediately qualified by '[that we] . . . may walk by the light of faith,/and serve you in newness of life' (p.217); all of which petitions have good Scriptural precedent.
[5] 'By the power of your life-giving Spirit bless these waters of your new creation.'
[6] The act of dedication is a lightly adapted version of one published in the Canadian *Book of Alternative Services,* 1985. The version published in *The Promise of His Glory* is also to be found in *Patterns for Worship,* p.135.
[7] See also Chapter V. C. section 30, p.221. This rubric also indicates that alternatively, the water may be 'placed in vessels by the door for . . . [the worshippers] to make the sign of the cross as they leave, or poured out over the threshold'.

The themes of the Church's mission and unity are provided for in Chapter V. D. 4 and 5. These suggestions could be further supplemented by material from the CCBI and CTE,[1] and from other denominations, as appropriate. On pp.245-6 it is worth noting the imaginative endings to a service for the mission of the Church. These are drawn from a number of sources[2], and all have the nature of a strong commissioning to proclamation and service as the people depart.

THE PRESENTATION OF CHRIST IN THE TEMPLE
The feast of the Presentation of Christ in the Temple (often referred to in *The Promise of His Glory* under its medieval title of 'Candlemas') is treated in *Promise* as the final culmination of the Christmas/Epiphany season. It is described as

'an important turning point in the Christian year . . . It is as if we say, on 2 February, "One last look back to Christmas, and now, turn towards the cross!"' (p.259).

Sundays after Candlemas are deemed to be 'before Lent'. Such is the pivotal significance of this feast in the calendrical provision of *The Promise of His Glory* that encouragement is given[3] to celebrate the feast on the nearest Sunday to February 2 so that its impact is not lost on worshippers.

This feast is fundamentally a Christological one: the child proclaimed and celebrated in the Temple is the one born to die. This bittersweet gospel is reflected in vigil and eucharistic provision for the feast. Musically, such themes might be enhanced by the use of one or two Christmas carols, alongside hymns or songs centred on the cross. 'The Lord is present in his sanctuary'; 'Within the veil'; 'Thou who wast rich beyond all splendour'; 'The holly and the ivy'; When Jesus Christ was yet a child'; these amongst others demonstrate the range of music which could be used on this feast.

In its medieval development, the feast attracted Marian devotions through its association with Jewish rites of female purification following childbirth. The old liturgies began with a procession with candles which seem to have had a Marian and penitential feel. The notion of a procession has been retained in the provision of *The Promise of His Glory*, but its preferred position[4] is now at the end of the eucharistic rite. The procession is simply a means of departure, with a sober tone being struck by the singing or recitation of a suitable version of the Nunc Dimittis. Unless the congregation is processing out to a church hall it is, only realistic to expect that their candles may be extinguished well before the final responsory at section 35, p.282!

---

[1] Council of Churches for Britain and Ireland (CCBI); and Churches Together in England (CTE).
[2] In particular, the Liturgical Commission has drawn on Celtic traditions developed in the worship of the Iona Community.
[3] Chapter VI. A, p.261, note 1.
[4] Chapter VI. C. section 34.

5. THE SAINTS AND THE DEAD

by Michael Vasey

Chapter II of *Promise* consists mainly of forms or prayer for three special days in November: All Saints Day, the Commemoration of the Faithful Departed, and Remembrance Day.[1] In places where these have a high profile they create a mood in which people's thoughts turn naturally to the joyful state of the Christian dead and to their own sense of frailty and loss.

Some may view these events as 'exotics', forms of ecclesiastical or civic self-indulgence that are are 'high-church', morbid and nationalist. They can also be viewed as opportunities which address one of the great pastoral issues of our time, namely people's ignorance of and confusion about life after death. Many studies have shown that church people, even strong 'biblical-believing' Christians, have little clear understanding in this area.

People's views of death and life after death are formed by the way society and church handle them. Secular silence about death is paralleled by a reticence in many evangelical churches, where there is little in ordinary Sunday worship to strengthen people's grasp of the presence of the Christian dead with Christ 'in the realm of light' (Col. 1.12). 1 Corinthians 15. St. Paul's great chapter on the resurrection, was written to counter Christian scepticism about the after-life (cf. v.12.19). In Jesus's day the Sadducees dismissed the Pharisees' clear beliefs about future life as unwarranted speculation that was not based on any clear scriptural teaching. Jesus and Paul sided unambiguously with the Pharisees (Luke 20.27-38, Acts 23.6-8, 24.14). Many modern Christians, including 'thoughtful' evangelicals, take a position closer to that of the Sadducees.

There are many signs that this cultural silence about death is breaking up. CRUSE and the bereavement counselling movement have an important part in this. Tony Walter's important book *Funerals And How To Improve Them* calls for a radical rethink, not least by the Church of England.[2] Reshaping people's grasp on life after death cannot simply be left to funerals. All Saints and 'All Souls' can play a part in this.

As with much other material in *Promise* there is no need to adopt a ceremonious or 'catholic' style. Much of it can be used very effectively in informal contexts and with quite different cultural dress.

All Saints Day

New Testament thought about the state of the believing dead moves between two poles. One voice speaks of people being 'with the Lord' (2

[1] *The Order for Remembrance Sunday* owes nothing to the Liturgical Commission; it is an ecumenically agreed form published on the authority of the Archbishops.
[2] Hodder 1990. See also the important Douglas J. Davies *Cremation Today and Tomorrow* (Grove Books, Bramcote 1990).

Cor. 5.8), 'reigning in life' (Rom. 5.17), 'citizens of the new Jerusalem' (Heb. 12.22-24, Phil. 3.20, Rev. 6.9-11, 7.13ff., 14.1-5). The other voice looks to a final moment of vindication and resurrection (Luke 13.23-30, Phil. 3.21, Rev. 19.21, possibly 2 Tim. 1.18). The table-fellowship of the eucharist embodies both strands; it expresses both present fellowship and also the 'marriage-supper' (Rev. 19.9) to come.

All Saints Day probably means for most Anglicans the superb hymn 'For all the saints'. *Promise* suggests that the First Sunday in November be kept as a Sunday in All Saints' tide. It includes old and new material which is perhaps better explored than discussed! It encourages a sense of communion with those in heaven without tipping over into controversial ideas of intercession.[1]

Commemoration of the Faithful Departed
This careful title is also usually used in the ASB, although it is once called by its more popular and controversial name 'Commemoration of All Souls' (p.20). Within the history of the church this day of commemoration has been fraught with difficulty.[2] It had its distant origin in the human desire and need to mark both the passing of loved persons and their continuing place in the affection of those near them. Early Christians, like Jews, followed the funeral with occasions when they remembered their loved ones in prayer. This, of course, is not the same as petitionary prayer directed to altering the state of the person who has died.

Promise offers two orders of service, a eucharist for November and a non-eucharistic form of memorial service. It is not an attempt to revive ideas of purgatory (a 'place' where imperfect *believers* are cleansed for heaven) or of any notion of changing the state of the dead (see discussion below). It does seek to provide an occasion when people can bring their love and their sense of loss to God. It consists of readings and prayers which relate to these feelings.

Two places are provided in the eucharist when the names of those who have died can be remembered: during the prayers or in the quiet after communion. Again the style need not be 'catholic' or formal. People can be invited to come forward, name a person and light a candle. Graham Kendrick's song 'Jesus stand among us at the meeting of our lives' fits well.

Prayer and the Departed
The following points attempt to make clear how the services in *Promise* have handled this controversial issue.

1. By the time of the Reformation prayer *for* the departed was linked inexorably with the purging of imperfect Christians in purgatory, and with the idea of the eucharist as a sacrifice offered to put away the sins of the living

---

[1] An indispensable book for thinking through these issues is Michael Perham's *The Communion of Saints* (Alcuin/SPCK 1980, 1983).

[2] Michael Perham discusses the issues very informatively, through from a stance which will not always be congenial to evangelicals. For the history and modern Roman Catholic understanding of the day see A. Adam *The Liturgical Year* (Pueblo, NY, 1981) pp.237-240.

and the dead. The Reformers saw in these a denial of the achievement of Calvary and of justification, and also a device by which a priestly caste came between human beings and God. Their response was to reject categorically any reference to the dead in prayer save general statements about a resurrected state. The 1662 Book of Common Prayer upheld this position while introducing (in the Prayer for the Church Militant) an 'us with them' reference to the Christian dead.

This drastic remedy rooted out a great error but at the price of leaving no voice for the love of the bereaved and of changing the post-Protestant funeral from something done *for* the person who has died to something for the bereaved. One of the first evangelicals to question this policy was Handley Moule.[1]

2. The traditional controversy was entirely about prayer for the Christian dead. The rise of nineteenth century scepticism and the collapse of Christendom have raised a different issue: prayer for those who have professed no faith in Christ. This is probably the nerve-centre of current evangelical concern with this issue. People fear that any such prayer denies that salvation comes only through Jesus Christ or—a different objection—undermines the urgency of response.

There may be some confusion in this position. To say that Jesus is the only way to the Father does not necessarily mean that only those who profess faith in Christ are saved through him (cf. the publican of Luke 18.9-14). 'Just people made perfect' (Heb. 12.23, cf.11.40) makes this explicit for believers of the Old Testament era and may imply the same for others who also 'desire a better country' (Heb. 11.16). A similar thought is present in the petition 'Hasten the day . . .' in section 16 of the All Saints service which picks up Luke 13.29, (cf. Acts 10.34). (This in turn does not imply either that everyone will be saved—a view apparently excluded by e.g. Luke 13.24, John 5.29—or that response in this life is not decisive, cf. Luke 16.19ff, Heb. 9.27).

In judging the pastoral priority it needs to be remembered that many congregations include first generation Christians from other religious and ethnic backgrounds.

3. The position in modern Church of England services can be traced to two events. The first is Colin Buchanan's dissent in 1966 from petitions for the departed in the Series 2 Communion Service.[2] This established that modern services must take evangelical conviction seriously. The second was the 1971 Doctrine Commission Report *Prayer and the Departed* which proposed a number of liturgical texts to achieve this end. The most creative appears as §13 in the ASB funeral rite and in I. D§16 of *Promise:*

> 'May God in his infinite love and mercy bring the whole Church living and departed in the Lord Jesus to a joyful resurrection and the fulfilment of his eternal kingdom.'

It could be used to conclude prayer in other contexts.

[1] See *Prayer and the Departed* (SPCK, 1971) pp.88-89.
[2] C. O. Buchanan *Recent Liturgical Revision in the Church of England* (Grove Books, Bramcote, 1973) pp.19, 26, 34.

INTRODUCING PROMISE OF HIS GLORY

Two further developments are worthy of note. One is the addition of 'according to your promises' (cf. Rite A §21, penultimate petition) which we owe to Hugh Craig. The second is the phrase towards the end of the ASB litany, 'both those who have confessed the faith and those whose faith is known to you alone'.

4. The Book of Common Prayer Order for the Visitation of the Sick provides a commendatory prayer 'for a sick person at the point of departure'. The ASB funeral rite includes a form of commendation. The Commemoration services in *Promise* assume a distinction between prayer that is appropriate *at* the time of death and prayer *after* death. The prayer at D. 34 is adapted from a prayer in the Book of Common Prayer of the Episcopal Church. It is intended to refer back confidently to the commendation at the time of death and thus avoid any suggestion of continuing petition for the person who has died. (Compare also 'enfold' in E. 11.)

The traditional Orthodox contakion is included at D. 33 on the ground that it conforms to the 'us with them' pattern of the BCP and comes from a *milieu* untainted by the errors of the late medieval West. Some may be less happy with the unqualified prayers in E. 4 and E. 12 and may wish to accept the Preface's invitation to pastoral adaptation.

These services are not determinative for the doctrine of the Church of England. Judgments about whether they are useful will involve balancing the pastoral needs of the grieving with any danger that faith in Jesus' decisive victory over death is undermined by their use.